THE MYTHS OF NATIVE TREES AND OTHER POEMS

Other Books by Ian Gouge

Novels and Novellas

The Opposite of Remembering - Coverstory books, 2020

At Maunston Quay - Coverstory books, 2019

An Infinity of Mirrors - Coverstory books, 2018 (2nd ed.)

Losing Moby Dick and Other Stories - Coverstory books, 2017 (2nd ed.)

The Big Frog Theory - Coverstory books, 2018 (2nd ed.)

Short Stories

Degrees of Separation - Coverstory books, 2018

Secrets & Wisdom - Paperback, 2017

Poetry

First-time Visions of Earth from Space - Coverstory books, 2019

After the Rehearsals - Coverstory books, 2018

Punctuations from History - Coverstory books, 2018

Human Archaeology - Paperback, 2017

Collected Poems (1979-2016) - Paperback, 2017

Anthologies

Triple Measures - Coverstory books, 2020

Oak Tree Alchemy - Coverstory books, 2019

Ian Gouge

The Myths of Native Trees and Other Poems

Coverstory books

First published in paperback format by
Coverstory books, 2020

ISBN 978-1-9162899-0-1

Copyright © Ian Gouge 2020

The right of Ian Gouge to be identified as
the author of this work has been asserted by
them in accordance with the Copyright,
Designs and Patents Act 1988.

For details on the cover image, please see
the Acknowledgements section.

All rights reserved.

No part of this publication may be
reproduced, circulated, stored in a system
from which it can be retrieved, or
transmitted in any form without the prior
permission in writing of the publisher.

www.iangouge.com

www.coverstorybooks.com

Contents

The Myths of Native Trees

Alder	7
Ash	8
Aspen	9
Birch	10
Cherry	11
Elder	12
Elm	13
Hawthorn	14
Hazel	15
Holly	16
Juniper	17
Oak	19
Scots Pine	20
Rowan	21
Willow	22
Yew	24

The Myths of History

At 'Friar's Crag', Boxing Day, 2018	29
Railway Vignettes	30
Protest	32
Ripon Cathedral, A Bright Morning	34
A Piccadilly Bookshop	36
The Mailbox	37
Tell-tale Footprints	38
A York Weekend	39
Full English on the 6:17	40
Curtain	41
Analysis	42
Cinders	43
After the Concert	44
For Liz Darby	46
A Candle, Guttered	47
Reading Between the Lines	48
Antique	49
The Crucible	50
Erosion	51
News	52
Grief	53

Letting Go	54
Re-reading Larkin	55
Restoration	56
Entree	57
The Road	58
In The Snug	59
Shrouded	60
Carnivore	61
Taste	62
Transit Camp	63
Night Passage	64
Trapped	65
Notebooks	66
Hide	68
Brachiation	69
The Calling	70
Looking for Shelter	72
Vocal	Chords	74

Not 'The Sonnets'

The Seasons (#2)	79
Pilgrimage (#7)	80
In Mourning (#9)	81
Orienteering (#13)	82
Late Frost (#18)	83
Slam, Vulnerable (#24)	84

❖

Acknowledgements	87

*for the skill, wit and wisdom of my
friends in the North Yorkshire and
Derby Stanza groups*

The Myths of Native Trees

Alder

in a forest   green is no camouflage

we sought refuge
                concealment
mistaken in our naïve belief
hiding beneath the alders' canopy
        our secret
                our elopement
would remain hidden

away from the trail
the heavy ground slowed our escape
and later
        mired ankle-deep in water
we understood why some paths
                      are seldom trodden

in a forest   green is no camouflage

Ash

"my passion is animals" you said
        your voice in the mid-distance
            off-hand
      as if it belonged somewhere else
          to someone else

"the serpent and the eagle" you said
        after I queried your favourites
"they are full of insight and wisdom"
        your voice betraying a longing
           for something mystical or magical
              of another place

"did you know" you said
"from the antlers of a deer
sprang the rivers of the world?
that the serpent and the eagle
protect the purity of springs?"

        I was always confused in your world
           as if it were not my home

"you belong in the underworld" you nearly said
        watching me as I fashioned
          spears from the bough of an ash
              then concentrating
                took aim

Aspen

in the deep silence of the woods
murmurings
and the kindness of the dead
cocooned about me
as if all they knew had become my shield
unseen protectors
guardians of body and soul

I walk reverently
slowly
allowing my feet to gently riffle
through fallen leaves
as if leaves are all that's left of them

Birch

furred by freezing fog
the landscape waits nervously
for the emergence of spring
as if it were a promise
never guaranteed

sitting in an attic bedsit
he reads about witches
and how broomsticks are made
as if both were real
he reads about potential
about love and renewal
and dreams of goddesses who might rescue him
driving out the daemons
who feed on winter solitude

in the sky
the moon lingers
elbowing its way into the day
as if to prove a point
we give it names
in recognition of its importance
and our subservience
      blood
            blue
                  wolf
                        worm
but never spring

Cherry

in the tree
the cuckoo watches
as the bough
              bends
with a force it never knew it had
to kiss the hand of a woman
heavy with her own fruit

the bird has no song for this
and feels
       for the first time
an interloper

silently it unfurls its feathers
and moves on

Elder

after supper
you waited at the back door
to prevent my leaving

it made me laugh
your taking this stand
eyes slightly wide
the mildly narcotic look
of a scared fawn

I admired your bravery
and the passionate way
you insisted elder
made the best instruments

as if to prove a point
your playing was dextrous
divine
a rapture to keep me secure
protected from myself

I did not see him at first
but rather a shadow
swinging over your shoulder
even as that tune you'd played
continued on a never-ending loop
heavenly inside my head

Elm

when fear triumphs over patience
victory can be shocked in a moment
a loss that cannot be undone

it is no matter that Orpheus' song
could vanquish the underworld
when weakness and uncertainty
turns everything to shade

the trees that guard these graves
were once more than solemn way-marks
and navigators for the forlorn
gnarled
they are no longer blessed
wood for a god-gifted lyre
now warped
to rob the living of music's mythic charm

Hawthorn

(for David McAndrew)

if there had been such a tree
quietly rampant in your garden
would you   seduced by its blossom
have severed a cluster
to decorate your home

I doubt it

I would not have been surprised
to find your knowledge stretched
beyond the soft verge of folklore
and superstition
yet it was neither curse nor bad luck
that led you away

in a final twist of fate
you may have welcomed
this other less visible blooming
the reward for an unshakeable belief in myth
freedom to embrace your beloved Anne
once more

Hazel

beheaded and gutted
the salmon simmers in the pan
its light brown spots
discoloured by splattering butter

where is your wisdom now

stand at the pool's edge and watch
always at the periphery of sight
ripples
and beneath the silver waves
mythical fish feed
on the gift of the hazel tree

"caught owt today, Jack?"

"nay; them fish's far too canny"

or almost always

living betrays the myth
and the chef
licking his butter-sweetened thumb
feels as if he has inherited
the wisdom of the ages

Holly

he was a giant of a man
ruler of darkness
and when he moved
more in the shadows than not
fear followed

radiance and colour
were the gloss on his protection racket
while you
happy to turn a blind eye to stay safe
would sing his praises
even as you wished for spring
and his overdue hibernation

if it were possible
for witches to have their own myths
he would be there
four-square before them
threat and challenge
and nemesis

decorating the house for Christmas
you prick your finger
the bulb of your blood
red like a berry

Juniper

we had become all calculation
governed by the calendar   and cycles

> in wanting something so much
> we had forced it to retreat
> overwhelmed by our onslaught

I resorted to research
to mythology   and old wives' tales

we played a game   word association
and when I said "juniper"
> you   quick as a flash
> > "gin"

I smiled
you said "what"

your eyes left mine
glancing to where they could burrow
through the wall to the casket of the fridge
to see if there was lemon there

> I saw the computation of volume
> of days since opening
> and whether there would be fizz
> left in the tonic
> > or fizz in my tonic

you had your doubts
    unlike Herod
        from whom Jesus was hidden
            beneath a tree

juniper
infuser of gin
symbol of fertility
shelter for prophets

Oak

more symbol than object
we know what it means
before we know how it looks

solid
dependable
if you are a native
       it's our mythology

yet if you say 'crown'
people conjure laurel and Romans
or thorns
       - and Romans again

"ah oak" you say
"the king of trees"

vulnerable to lighting strikes
and invasion by mistletoe
they are giants brought low
       by fire
              and love

Scots Pine

there is a whisper in the air
        silence-pure
a mountain breeze caresses
attentive leaf-bound boughs
        swaying regally

picking a cone from the ground
you wonder aloud if they have always been there
these trees
        these cones

"if you take one home
does it open and close with time?"

obscurely
I am reminded of your heart
and love's inconstancy
and know I cannot answer

Rowan

when I found I loved you
a word was all I needed
a syllable to capture how my heart felt
eagle-soaring

when I found I loved you
I was potion-drunk
lips kissing the golden chalice
of life's nectar

when I found I loved you
words were my bind
the hollow drug for a tortured soul
hopelessly enchanted
because I found I loved you

Willow

on the river
the moon reflected
      fractured and rebuilt
      by the movement of the water
            only to be fractured and rebuilt again

in the summer-evening still
apologies for waves
lap at the punt

it feels poetic
as if ancient others
transported here
would be able to wane
more graciously than the moon

is this the stuff of power
and immortality
      the prize of being able to create
           something immutable

in the empty boat
his hands freeze
      the water on the pole
      especially cold tonight

he passes the willow overhang
where once he was entangled
and she laughed

misfortune or ineptitude
he cannot decide
knowing only that he feels
more vulnerable than before
      hearing her laughter in the lapping water
      seeing her eyes in the shattered reflection
           of the broken moon

Yew

its softness surprises
hard edges chamfered
to a caress

perhaps it is the colour
its darkness
the way it captures light

       not all prisons
       are made of bars

this hedge has succeeded generations
sculpted by innumerable gardeners
their peacocks and their rabbits
the most enduring of the species

*

The Myths of History

At 'Friar's Crag', Boxing Day, 2018

we saw the flowers first
tied hurriedly askew to a low fence
less fence than coarse attempt
to keep us to the rocky path
the path from where we saw the dust
not dust but pale grey ash
less scattered than smuggled
like an escape-tunnel digger's
tip and run under cover of night
their loved one reunited with a favoured haunt
a place where now they lie
unprotected from the elements
they once embraced
to which they must finally succumb

they will be gone tomorrow
nothing left
but the flowers we saw first

Railway Vignettes

1
sheep lie in a field
there   a black one
another   and again
the rogue family of the estate

across the frosted hedgerow
the scar of a cavernous hole
a burial mound inverted
and silent diggers poised
in their uniform yellow
waiting for the day to start
like sheep in a field

2
the guard announces Burton-on-Trent
in bouncing sing-song
as if it's Torremolinos or some chart-topping destination
to which all your tracks have been leading

it isn't of course
but rather a nondescript place
with areas of posh and not
and huge brewery funnels
pumping the aroma of beer
into clean spring air

3
she limps as she walks
not because her trolley bag
black and trailing behind her
like a vaguely obedient dog
is especially heavy
nor because she is overweight (she is)
or her tights are laddered (they are)

she looks out of kilter
her hair uncombed   apologetic
as if it has already been a long day

she looks as if she wants
to be leaving   again
but she is just arriving
limping as she does

4
a woman sits with her son
and silently contemplates
the accidents of history
she wishes she could undo
as easily as slipping
a ring from a finger
as if that would free her
'til life us do part
free to go searching
for the things she lost
or the things she believes
have passed her by
like vignettes seen through
a railway carriage window

Protest

the banners were hand-made
crafted from garage leftovers
and worn out felt-tips   or their kids' ancient painting sets
letters shadowed in highlighter orange
       for emphasis   and fire
              colours running in the rain
they stole incendiary chants from the terraces
recycled   repurposed

the uniformed looked on   passive
as if nothing to do with them
unconnected bystanders
out for a stroll with their mates
in kevlar   just in case

in the drizzle some heads were hot
blinded by their cause
shackled by the impotence of their words

they shouted   their placards shouted
but no-one listened

an onlooker smoked languidly
and in a shop doorway a photographer
searched for an angle that would look perfect
in black-and-white
       waiting   in case it all kicked off

people moved slowly   or didn't move at all
tension taut like an elastic band
about   to   snap

a cry   the holding of breath
then from the back   an arm enflamed   swung

years later
the BBC voice-over has become legend
its words the narrative
      of the struggle
           the conflict
                the outcome
and the black-and-white photo
of a uniform smeared with blood
      something motionless on the ground
           is a fable
                or the only truth

the following weekend in bright sunlight
keepers in smart peaked caps   kits vibrant
the local derby a one-all draw
                and the pubs all full again

Ripon Cathedral, A Bright Morning

in the sharp early light
soft tones of muted stone
drowned by the clash between light and shade
all hard edges   blades to cut yourself on

stark against a sky paint-tube blue
it towers over you
threatening

there may be collateral damage
Cezanne versus Dali
                     or Good versus Evil
inside
air calm and cool
as if charmed by hidden forces
pumped with harmony   peace
        mythic things you read about
              or dream of
inside
has banished the harsh
sunlight suffused into rainbow-colours
playing like well-behaved children

sit a while

it becomes your familiar
the confidant you never knew you had
nonsense about hard lines
and the threat of black shadow
not even a memory

sit a while   and breathe
absorb the day   yourself
       the potential of yourself

you would pray if you could

instead
you nod toward the altar window
and then quietly retreat
past the unmanned perspex chest

    three pounds per head donation please

and out
for another shot at redemption

A Piccadilly Bookshop

In the calm of this oasis
away from Eros' roar
and the hot scrum of confusion
café sentences are batted to and fro,
polite baseline rallies
across the net of china's clink.
Uncertain what to write
a man stares at multi-coloured pens,
hand poised above untroubled sheets;
and there, a woman regains her husband,
her books secured, brandished like a trophy.
Students pore over laptops
and diligently shared pastries,
surrounding themselves with wisdom,
hoping it will bleed from the shelves
into furtively typing fingers.
Huddled businessmen compare notes,
re-articulating closet deals,
whispers as combative as suits and ties.

Outside, beyond the plate-glass guard,
a wild-eyed tramp soundlessly berates a tourist
unconscious of his filth and lack of socks,
adamant that what he knows
is an unvarnished slice of all our truths.

The Mailbox

glitz is expensive
back-lit letters above shuttered store-fronts
hiding pristine interiors
boasting the impossibly perfect

people queue outside
lusting for names
to add to their collection

Boss
Hilfiger
Gieves & Hawkes

I acquiesce to well-heeled covetousness
choosing to take coffee here
over New Street Station bistros
where you risk rudimentary encounters
perhaps the man at the public urinal
muttering to himself
and shouting at the world
so recently wrapped in unbranded blanket
and pavement-dwelling
not a million miles from here

Tell-tale Footprints

her feet betray her
the wrinkles of parchment skin   the proud veins
like tracings on a map
the catalogue of her journey

when he left her unexpectedly
he stole the spring from her step

now memory matches her stride

become longer than ever
their old route round the park
and after
sitting with her feet up
muscles complaining
in ways they never had before

now she merely strolls
forgiving the aches   the pains
the price of wisdom

embraced by soft leather
they are reconciled
like old friends reunited
their falling-out no more than misunderstanding

A York Weekend

(with apologies to Philip Larkin)

The station spews them out,
in lurid shades and orange spray
tan-tottering towards Happy Hours
designed to last all day.

Over-stilettoed and
squeezed into unforgiving fabric
they crease and wobble into town
in search of something magic;

eyes Egyptian-painted
deifying inebriation,
steeped in alcohol inside-out
ripe for mummification.

Coarse accents echo across a river
that embraces misstepped revelling
and those trying to beat the odds
or land a touch on spread betting;

and later they will dribble
spent onto the Knavesmire,
a plastic wave of humanity
in celebrity-copycat attire.

Betrayed by anti-climax,
staggering, they shout,
piss in hedges, puke on lawns,
hollowed and emptied by a great day out.

Full English on the 6:17

Breakfast en route to London
everything so hot
you can almost taste the radiation.

Across the First Class aisle
a young woman in a too-short hooped dress
watches videos on her phone
self-consciously out of place.
And grey commuters
whose days blur into an amalgam of routine
take their usual seats
and pay homage to the ritual,
a daily grind that starts and ends
with the alarm clock.

"Coffee please. And Full English."

The bacon tasted a little like processed cardboard,
yet who would have thought
black pudding could symbolise refinement?

Satisfied,
I sit back in my individual airline-style seat
and watch the black world
skitter by outside
waiting for the sun to rise.

Curtain

between the valley and the peak
fragments of light sliding through the clouds
flicker like scraps of confetti
easily slipped into stillness

breathing hard through an open smile
his eyes see with specific literacy
ancient waterfalls carving in slow motion
a ribbon of majestic beauty
one side of a mortal veil
drifting like a cobweb in the air

Analysis

Voices rise to no more than a whisper;
conversation comes with a note of caution.
Is this a fear of the present
or trepidation at the rumours of beatings,
the internment of freedoms?

You shrug your shoulders, knowing
ghost stories lay hidden behind history.

Interpreting the past is a skill,
like reading between narrow lines
or being able to watch clumsy swans
learning organically how to land.

Bombarded with facts, you shun
the school-yard view of performance,
wary of conclusions, especially when
we don't know where the truths are.

Cinders

when we had money
we would bank-up the fire overnight
some priceless coal
and shovelfuls of cinders
saved from previous days

when we were lucky
the fire would still be glowing
in the morning
coaxed back to life
with a few scraps of wood

when unlucky
at least the room would be warm
even if the ritual
of saving the spent embers
needed to be reinitiated

turning money into cinders
watching it go up in smoke
in exchange for heat
was temporary respite
for a small child

After the Concert

falling foul of memory's snare
the fragile recollection
of an evening when time crept
so slowly
it felt as if we owned it
as if the moon
would never break beyond the branches
of that winter ash

it was romantic I suppose
but I
confused
was torn between longings
for time to crawl
so that I could hold you there
for time to race
that I might hold you breathless elsewhere

lately it is not time I recall
but the chill of the night
the cold of the fire-escape rail
on my empty hands
the dull thumping from the concert hall
the tremolo of my heart

in prescient mood
even then I knew what would come
later that night
and the next when you gently let me down

the moon passes beyond the ash
illumination of a fragment of time
the varnish and shadow
of a passing moment

For Liz Darby

fifty years since

years smuggled almost illegally
disguising themselves
        with incident   accident   crisis
and from nowhere I am reminded of
an effervescent girl
who laughed as if she were party to secrets
        kept from the rest of us
who courted scandal with short skirts
        and being the first to wear a bra
who took me to the park that sunny Saturday
        and introduced me to my first wet kiss

I have been guilty all these years
for the way I cast you aside
a twelve-year-old's fear victorious over everything

how wistful is this
recognising at the other end of time
how much life you owned
        and how much of it you offered me

A Candle, Guttered

betrayed by this soft groove
a fountainhead melted in hot light
its bequest   an uneven trail
pale witness of lives
traded for a compendium of importance
or of trivia   perhaps

did we realise
or were we seduced by such moments
our testimonies compiled from fragments
like a seed-cloud
airborne in a ripe dandelion field

perhaps one seed settled
      here   or here
an idea given the chance to root
and begin the cycle again

perhaps   in the candlelight
we talked about dandelions
and what weeds were
no more   you said   than ideas growing
where they were not wanted

I thought of our past
and what had separated us
and how a guttered candle
might tell the story

Reading Between the Lines

silhouettes painted by your words
blurred outlines from shared events
like looking through a mirror from the wrong side

truth hides in the corners of the glass
obscured by metallic blooming
camouflaged at the ends of a rainbow
       to avoid capture

how long has it been on the run

we deconstructed the known to find meaning
only to lose it again
like an inadequate bookmark
slipped deep within the folds
of an antiquarian prize
written in a forgotten tongue

disappointed
I trust only my own eyes
watching dancing ghosts blend
      with the fictional
           the might-have-beens

Antique

I wanted you to bleed on the page
the ink of your words   lifeblood
testament to the past we shared

I wanted to feel the heat of you
betraying perspective   giving form
to the other side of my story

instead
a wound key animates a music box devoid of sound
its figure pirouetting without grace
in a mechanical display

here is a music box you say
as if that is enough

then leaving me in the vacuum of the past
you remove the key
and drop it carefully into your waistcoat pocket

The Crucible

Separated by no more than a regulation red
or a short-range pot into a corner pocket
we sat eating sandwiches and drinking coke,
staring down on the amphitheater
as if waiting for something to happen.
The semi-hush was reverential.

I had arrived at your side amateur-like
hope out-playing talent
uncertain of my accomplishments
and whether I was ready for the big stage.

In truth I'd never had a chance,
always misreading your angles,
defeated by the nap of the cloth.

If it seemed to matter then
it is no more than illusion now,
relegated to the black-and-white replay
of a one-sided encounter
missing the frame-saving ball,
the applause of the crowd,
a break into the big time.

Erosion

the pebbled beach
a congregation celebrating
the tribulation of tides
smoothed to impossible ellipses
that beg to be spun back out to sea
as if relaunched into their past

and I wonder how the tides have worked on you
corrupting your once unblemished surface
each wave-clash sending blade-sharp shards
dangerous through the air

what was it shaped you
to become the dark flint
firing sparks from our past

News

I wait for the telephone to ring.
The inevitability of it.
This is a strange waiting,
a long waiting
              wishing for something not to happen
     even though it must.

I tried your line today.
My turn to call.
There was nothing after the dialling tone
as if that was the end of it,
                            nothing more
                                          nothing left.
For a moment it was liberating.

Grief

there is a space where you used to be

I see it on grey station platforms
and in shuffling supermarket aisles

strange how it is never occupied
                              despite the throng

I feel it during countryside walks
my hand abandoned
constantly surprised to find yours
                              not there

a voice   lost like me   asks
not why you are not here
                          but why am I

and why do I bother to make that journey
      or go to work
           or read this book

they say all stories have two sides

if that is true
then I am living half of ours
staring at the space you once filled

Letting Go

an entrance through rough scrub
leads to unmapped landfill
poorly disguised behind forlorn hedgerows
scant welcoming for birds

rutted tracks betray the trespassers
who come in darkness
to divest themselves of the unwanted
sloughing off flakes of veneer
as if they were snakes shedding skin

my car steers erratically
its narrow wheelbase a mismatch
for deep and puddled ruts
skimming the mud's crust
its chassis gouging my progress
like a tell-tale tracing
on a well-worn map

parked beside a buckled mattress
I unload today's modest offering
      part-read classics
         the corpse of an unkept diary
           a notebook whose last few naked pages
              seem beyond salvation

tossing them into the blackness
should feel like a release
but they are greeted by silence
like sacrifices looking for a cause

Re-reading Larkin

All the while I can sense him
looking over my shoulder
as if marking my homework,
a dubious figure in a grubby raincoat
loitering at the back.
Is that expression the resentment
he has to loiter there at all
or merely suburban anger at time
wasted on me?

Annoyed at the intrusion
he tuts under his breath
as he might a noisy bookworm.

'How many more fucking times
do I need to tell you?'

Waving a stubby pencil at a half-rhyme
he shakes his head
then shoulders his camera
determined to capture more of this miserable life
before it gets too late.

Left alone,
I weigh-up the merits of pairing
'blarney' with 'money'
and ask myself why *I* like to go into churches.

Restoration

scaffolding surrounds the church
ribs skeletal about the tower
its skin of rough tarpaulin hints
at Norman regularity and hidden fractures
      a cracked lintel
        gargoyles weather-worn
        glass more shattered than stained

inside
darkness triumphs over feeble candles
no matter how many are remembered
and where light should paint
rainbow shafts against memorial walls
nothing but a ghostly residue
like a confession's resonance
veneered against the curtained stall

memory whispers in the echo of your footfall
prompted too by damp stone and old oak pews
recalls school excursions with crayons and paper
searching for brasses upon which
to overlay an infant skill

out in the wind again
the loosely wrapped tarpaulin flaps
like Christmas paper slack around presents
you knew you were getting
      or emptily
        like all those hollow promises
        which remain unfulfilled

Entree

Twisting the facts
fuels subtle political shifts
and builds distance between us,
archipelago people unconnected by bridges.

In a village unsullied by 'news'
they make comfort food using natural ingredients,
recipes handed down through generations
tasting as good as ever.

Across the dinner table we dissect the menu
yet avoid questions of cultural identity
uncertain of our relative place
in the modest scheme of things.

A wry smile unwraps itself
at the notion of an outside world,
surfacing little relief in knowing
you are always part of someone else's story.

The Road

twists impossibly through granite
boasting the pretence of flatness

at points   at its darkest
it seems to double back
and confused by traitorous magnetism
throws awry the in-built compass
you claim to possess

seduced by the fakery of progress
that your goal   always after the next bend
will be revealed in a blaze of natural light
you press on
imagining you see a fragment
a sliver of brightness in the gloom

distance   or the illusion of distance
is a trade-off against depleting fuel
and promise's whisper

>*just around the corner*

yet still the darkness rolls on
the tank empties
and unseen   your hope bleeds too
a wound never to be staunched

In The Snug

The room was festive
flat surfaces over-decorated with cards
their brightness chiding the dark-panelled wood
more in benevolence than conflict.
You could be forgiven
for thinking you had strayed
into the left-overs of Christmas
or the remnants of a party held long ago.
Impervious to chatter from the bar
our hushed and intimate room
was breached only by a friendly mongrel
loosed from its lead.
As I waited
I pulled a card from the mantle
and was taken aback
by the words "In Sympathy".
Reading the shakily written inscription
I caught a sentence or two
before feeling like an intruder
who had casually gatecrashed
a memorial on hallowed ground.
Sobered by new context
I realised the sombre walls
held sway over these dabs of colour
tolerated for their muted reverence.
I replaced the card precisely
and took a sip from my cold dark beer.

Shrouded

in the gloom a headland bleeds to mist
colours running into grey
a wash as soft as any cheek-brushed kiss

a gull's abrasive scream
flies across the dunes then fades away
beckons to another yet unseen

scan the fluid shore for fractured clues
as each tide-tied pebble begs its say
in a puzzle dressed in camouflage fatigues

now beyond limp memory's fetch
and cloaked in out-of-focus overlay
history's fickle piper suggests a day

of breakers   sun-studded waves
a ballet of wind-blown marram swathes
and butterflies dancing in the vetch

Carnivore

You were always afraid of being bitten by a cow.
As if cows could bite
        or would masticate you to death.
You used to skirt the boundaries of fields
        always on the look-out
               everything at stake.
It was a fear that stripped conversation.
For a short while even beauty was out-flanked
filleted in an uneven fight for survival.

I think you were grateful
when your wandering days were over
and you could decline with practiced grace
invitations to walk in the countryside
and indulge more suitable passions
        like a recently developed penchant
              for sirloin
                     medium rare.

Taste

fashion is a colour   a cut
an idea new and fresh
that mimics evolution's challenge to the black-and-white

when dawn breaks   rosily
listen for the whisper
and remember the relics in the temple
statuary stained green with neglect

obsessed
we search
driven by glitz and 'best before'

       but I like the style   you say

people shake heads
defined by the selfie
and an urge to keep up
for those already too far behind

       but I like the tone   you say

and pityingly they mock
black is the new black
and walk away

Transit Camp

reverberations
heard through insubstantial doors
ghostly echoes of conversations on stark stairwells

in empty hallways
begrudgingly decked in antiseptic matting
      you meet no-one
trudge up one flight
laden with bags whose contents make no difference
unlock
      nineteen
decipher its tarnished lacquer
and wonder if that's what you've become
      a number

another sodden dawn births the unthinking routine
a soulless journey in a convoy of grey cars
      migratory to work
snarled in a blur of tail lights
you pay the penance
then the slog back
to an unwelcoming refuge
      working away from home

Night Passage

Flitting addictively between emotions
quiet imbalance has become an epidemic
a foil for the prescription used to manage life.
You search for medication to settle
the nervous twitch that turns recording into editing,
cements experience into long-term memories,
dusty volumes logged in a Dewey catalogue.

Once you believed in the ancient craft
and tried stitching a robe from haphazard scraps,
a gift as rare as a handwritten letter.
Exhausted by the effort, you find history
is a serpentine descent into an alternative world
rewarded by snatched dreams
where sometimes we believe we can fly.

All too late you discover sleep is a gift
denied to the insomniac and the guilty,
defined by something it is not.

Trapped

beneath the surface it shifts   restlessly
a vague presence betrayed by a meniscus swell
not even a ripple

no clinking chains restrain it
bound invisibly by tides
and the undercurrent drag
towards an ever-darker estuary

compelled   you try to give it form
imagine a shape   an amalgam
of everything you've ever known
animate   inanimate
it makes no difference

reluctant to give itself away
if it screams it does so silently
betraying emotions harvested from others' pain
and a compendium of all there is

sometimes   when the surface is still
you imagine it asleep
and close your eyes
glad to rest when it does

Notebooks

believing they could be extraordinary in technicolour
they lean nonchalantly
like forties screen icons reclined against soft focus backdrops
trying to own
                or disown
                              an image

they would wink at you if they could

surprisingly protective
they betray nothing of their secrets

slip one out   delicately
as if its contents might be fragile
and be struck by the domino effect
its neighbours closing ranks
as if space is a threat
and intimacy important

then open the cover and search
the pages   dated perhaps
adorned with   what
     scraps of narrative
     a complex idea set down in a simple phrase
     the early version of something you recognise

and here   coherent
a skeleton of the more substantial
articulated
bones wanting muscle

       muscle wanting flesh
            flesh wanting clothes
it had been exciting
               for a while

reverently you slip the book back
gaze at them all fondly

a little worn around the edges now perhaps
but in their black-and-white heyday

wow

Hide

Sleuth-like you scavenge for clues:
the roughness of bark to the touch,
a musky odour you can smell in the fog.

You imagine a slender, mouse-grey bird
and strive to describe it given only
the nocturnal song of one of its neighbours.

Undaunted, there is no option but
to go deeper in on a close summer night,
embracing a legend worth believing.

Absorbed in a cocoon of quiet industry
you find him watching and waiting,
perched in the blind, silently writing.

Brachiation

(brachiate vb. move by using the arms to swing from branch to branch)

a trunk   split
cleft in twisted two
gnarling upwards then cleft again   again
skyward soaring   bearing its children

> *come to us*
> *let us cradle you in our canopy of sinuous arms*

    and there   swinging
    the celebrants
    homage in their primordial cries
    knowing everywhere is home

❊

from word to liberated word
a poet sings
couched in a panoply
of meaning ever twisting

> *come to us*
> *let us caress you with our fragile leaves*

    and here   vellum-bound
    they celebrate all emotions
    hope in the face of failing
    of striving to touch the stars

The Calling

In drizzle-fuelled darkness
a fugitive epiphany hides as a spectre might,
crouching unseen in street-light shadows.
Betrayed, I lean on instinct
and feel the ebony dark,
desperate for connection,
groping for salvation.

Across the street   footfall
the innocent and anonymous of some other
simply walking,
talking to their phone
heading for a rendezvous
or a bus stop
or simply   back.

Tired of wandering,
I stand camouflaged in darkened doorways
hoping to catch it unawares,
catch it any way I can.
I hold my breath, still my heart.

I fear the consequence of failing
and wonder if those unmanned whisperings
- heard how many years ago? -
were just a ruse   a prank,
an idea implanted as a twisted joke
to torment me with falsehood,
the empty promise that something is waiting
something magical.

Vanquished and home again
I throw on the harsh porch light
and layer my shadow onto the world
while my life's promise
hides in the darkness
sniggering.

Looking for Shelter

Do you see the clouds?
They are dark and sombre,
threatening everything.
Strange how they appear
when your back is turned
or your attention diverted
sudden from the bluest sky
as if hiding all along,
wearing a perfect disguise.

They have a name, these clouds;
not cumulus-something
nor something-nimbus,
but a name much less meteorological
as if they have been cultivated from a scrapbook.
Or the Bible, perhaps.
Perhaps they are 'Lazarus clouds',
clouds I thought I'd seen the back of…

There are pills for clouds, did you know?
Small perfect little ovoids.
Perhaps they should be softer,
less well defined,
something you dissolve in water
- which would be far more appropriate.

These are not clouds for having your head in.
Quite the opposite.
And so I rummage through my word-sack
to take my mind off the weather;

I seek out small evaporations of sunshine
to try and repaint the sky
as if blue were my favourite colour.
Which it is not.

Vocal | Chords

I want a voice of my own. | A rasp like Dylan's -| two bars, you know it's him. | A voice is not what you say | but how you say it; | Dylan could wring agonies | from Mary and her little lamb. | If you spoke another language | you could still tell it was Dylan | or Sinatra. | Or Betjeman, come to that. | A voice exists beyond the words, | in the insubstantial spaces between them, | living the high-life in a parallel universe. | So I weave words on the page | to create a portal to another realm, | to connect to a sense beyond the surface, | braving all the self-scrutiny | to summon up the courage | to see if I can get there.

Not 'The Sonnets'

The Seasons (#2)

Do not mind my furrowed brow
ploughed naked like a frosted winter field;
you cannot soothe it now.
Do not believe these hands no longer held
were slick ministers of my lies,
but remember innocent and sultry days
when there was harvest in my eyes.

Neither vanity nor desperate self-praise
fuels this search for hollow words to use
as withered chaff now gilt as mine.
I do so openly and without excuse
to gather alms against the march of time;
these my only comfort when I'm frail and old
staring down the triumph of your bitter cold.

Pilgrimage (#7)

We set-off before first light
the pre-dawn drive straining the eye.
Numbed by pulsing headlights, my sight
tried to race ahead, to preview the majesty
of the village beneath the hill,
a return to a bygone age
where all we knew and loved remained there still.
It was a pilgrimage
even if we struggled in the car
and travelling wasted too much of the day.
"That's just the way things are"
you said. We were about halfway,
stopping for lunch at noon
already resigned to return too soon.

In Mourning (#9)

There used to be a sparkle in your eye
fired by a vigorous joust with life.
I watched it die
as I watched you lose your wife,
so desperate to weep
yet dry-eyed at being left behind.

She would have told you what to do: to keep
focused on the future,   your mind
alive,   sharply honed on how to spend
your time,   not waste it
as she feared she had at the end.

You say I cannot understand it,
how heavily it sits,
not death but the emptiness it commits.

Orienteering (#13)

The map offers no clues to where we are.
You'd said "let's get out and live!"
Enthusiasm robbed me of time to prepare,
ignorant of equations which balance give
and take, recognition that Life is on a lease.
You point to the plateau where we lately were,
tracing some vague and marginal decrease
as if the future is a hardship we can bear.
Seeking signposts, I find no decay
in your conviction, its mission to uphold
our cause, to challenge each day
grown more sullen as it grows cold.
How can I comprehend the truths you know,
unlock your faith in us that makes it so?

Late Frost (#18)

Surprised by the renegade day
you had expected the temperate,
a welcome more fitting for late May.

This chilled air has the tell of a first date
bound to fail.
                In the gathering grey nothing shines,
our prospects dimmed
as the dial's sharp shadow declines
with the sun.
                Sails untrimmed
you flounder and fade
becalmed into an all-consuming mist,
and leave nothing behind but the shade
and shape of one hoping to be kissed.

Robbed of the horizon, what's left to see
but life,
        still
                and frosted
                          and solitary?

Slam, Vulnerable (#24)

The future is steeled
against a plaintive heart.
The dearth of trump cards held
is testament to a dealer's art
and the slick-fingered skill
of skimming lies
from the bottom of the pack.
                    "Still"
you say, diamonds in your eyes,
"you're not quite done;
you might yet finesse me."

Ask me to eclipse the sun
or make spades from filigree;
both courses would be easier to chart
than triumph over the Queen of Hearts.

Acknowledgements

The cover image is a photograph taken by the author at Fountains Abbey, a World Heritage Site in North Yorkshire, UK.

Previous publications:
- "Pilgrimage" was first published in the online edition of *'The Aesthetic Apostle'*, February 2019
- "Alder", "Ash", "Birch", Cherry", "At 'Friar's Crag', Boxing Day, 2018", "Railway Vignettes", "Protest", "Re-reading Larkin", "Restoration", "Letting Go", "News", "Hide", "Curtain", "Night Passage", "A Candle, Guttered", "Erosion", "After the Concert", "Grief" and "Vocal | Chords" are also published in *'Triple Measures'*, by Miller, Gouge and Furniss, Coverstory books, 2020
- "Ripon Cathedral, A Bright Morning" was first published in 'Seeing Things', ed. Moor, Trewhitt and Turner, Ripon Poetry Festival, October 2019

www.ingramcontent.com/pod-product-compliance
Lightning Source LLC
Chambersburg PA
CBHW021120080526
44587CB00010B/578